THE TEN LA

LEGACY
AUTHOR

A Product of the True Vine Legacy
Author Wealth System

Timothy O Bond

www.truevinepublishing.org

The Ten Laws of the Legacy Author

Timothy O Bond

Published by

True Vine Publishing Co.

810 Dominican Dr.

Nashville, TN 37228

www.TrueVinePublishing.org

Printed in the United States of America—First printing.

INTRODUCTION

Why These Laws Exist

Writing a book is easy. Building legacy is not.

Many authors create with passion but lack structure. They write, publish, and hope something happens. When results do not come, they grow discouraged, distracted, or disappear entirely.

This book exists to bring order.

The Ten Laws of the Legacy Author are not motivational ideas. They are operating principles. They govern how you think, act, promote, invest, speak, and build. When followed, they remove confusion and replace it with direction.

These Laws are simple, but they are not optional. You cannot ignore service and expect impact. You cannot avoid visibility and expect growth. You cannot work alone and expect scale.

You do not need talent to follow these Laws. You need discipline.

This book is not meant to impress you. It is meant to guide you. Read it slowly. Return to it often. Measure yourself not by how inspired you feel, but by how faithfully you apply what is written.

Legacy is not built by accident. It is built by living under the Laws that govern it.

Law I
The Law of Service

A Legacy Author creates to serve.

———————— ✦ ————————

Law Statement:

I will create products and services
that serve others and improve lives.

If your book does not help someone, it will
not last. Readers may enjoy your words,
but they stay connected to work that solves a
problem or brings clarity. Service gives your
writing a reason to exist beyond expression.
It turns words into something useful.

When service is missing, the work often becomes centered on you instead of the
reader. Writing only to be seen, praised, or

understood leads to short lived results. Service shifts the focus outward. It asks who needs this message and how it can help them.

Serving the reader does not mean losing your voice. It means sharpening it. When you know who you are serving, your message becomes clearer. Your writing gains direction, and your purpose becomes easier to explain and share.

When service leads your work, impact follows. Readers trust you. Opportunities grow. Your book becomes more than a personal project. It becomes a tool that improves lives and carries your message further.

Law II
The Law of Alignment

*A Legacy Author governs the inner world
before the outer.*

———————————◆———————————

Law Statement:

I will govern my thoughts, beliefs, and
inner life before taking outward action.

When your thoughts are unsettled, your
actions become inconsistent. Doubt,
fear, and distraction often slow progress
before it even begins. Alignment brings order
to your thinking so that your actions are not
driven by emotion or pressure.

Without alignment, even good plans
feel heavy. You may start strong and then
lose focus. Inner disorder shows up as pro-

crastination, hesitation, or burnout. This Law exists to correct that pattern.

Alignment is built through intentional stillness. Time spent in reflection, prayer, meditation, or quiet thought allows you to reset your focus. It helps you hear what matters most instead of reacting to everything around you.

When your inner world is governed, your outer work becomes clearer. Decisions feel more grounded. You move forward with direction instead of force, and consistency becomes easier to maintain.

Law III
The Law of Execution

A Legacy Author does not delay destiny.

———————◆———————

Law Statement:

I will take consistent daily action toward
my goals regardless of how I feel.

Ideas alone do not build legacy. Planning
without action creates the illusion of
progress. Waiting for perfect conditions often
leads to nothing being done at all.

Execution is what separates intention
from outcome. Each day you delay, momentum fades. This Law exists to move you out
of waiting and into motion.

Small actions taken daily matter more than occasional bursts of effort. Writing one page, sending one message, or making one improvement compounds over time. Progress grows through consistency.

When you execute regularly, confidence builds. You stop doubting yourself because you see movement. Action clarifies direction and turns potential into reality.

Law IV
The Law of Daily Promotion

*A Legacy Author honors visibility as
responsibility.*

———————◆———————

Law Statement:

I will promote my work daily with
integrity and consistency.

A message that is never shared cannot
help anyone. Avoiding promotion may
feel comfortable, but it limits the reach of
your work. This Law exists to remind you
that visibility is part of service.

Promotion is not about ego. It is about
access. If people do not know your work exists, they cannot benefit from it. Hiding your
message does not protect it. It silences it.

Daily promotion keeps your work alive. It allows your message to stay in circulation and reach new people. Consistency builds familiarity and trust over time.

When you commit to daily promotion, growth becomes predictable. Your audience expands, opportunities increase, and your message gains momentum.

Law V
The Law of Investment

A Legacy Author invests where they expect growth.

——————— ✦ ———————

Law Statement:

I will invest my time, energy, and resources into my calling and my business.

What you refuse to invest in will not grow. Time, money, and attention reveal what you truly value. This Law challenges you to take your work seriously.

Avoiding investment often comes from fear. Fear of loss, fear of failure, or fear of commitment. This Law confronts hesitation and calls for responsibility.

Investment creates ownership. When you invest in your craft, systems, and support, you become more committed to the outcome. Growth requires sacrifice before it produces return.

The resources you invest today shape the opportunities you have tomorrow. Legacy is built by those willing to plant before they harvest.

Law VI
The Law of Declaration

A Legacy Author speaks outcomes before evidence.

---✦---

Law Statement:

I will speak success, clarity, and direction over my work and my future.

Your words shape how you think and act. Speaking doubt reinforces limitation. Speaking with intention strengthens direction. This Law governs how you talk about your future.

Silence or negative language weakens confidence. When you hesitate to speak clearly about where you are going, focus begins to drift. Direction becomes uncertain.

Declaration is not denial. It is commitment. Speaking outcomes helps anchor your actions and decisions, even when progress feels slow.

When your words align with your goals, your behavior follows. Clear declaration keeps you moving forward through uncertainty.

Law VII
The Law of Courage

A Legacy Author expands beyond comfort.

───────────◆───────────

Law Statement:

I will step outside of my comfort
zone to grow and advance.

Growth always requires discomfort.
New levels demand actions that feel
unfamiliar. Comfort preserves what already
exists, but it cannot create something new.

Fear often appears before progress.
Avoiding fear keeps you stuck in familiar
patterns. This Law exists to remind you that
discomfort is part of growth, not a reason to
stop.

Courage is built through action. Each step taken despite fear strengthens confidence. What once felt intimidating becomes manageable through experience.

When you choose courage consistently, opportunities open. Growth accelerates, and confidence increases through practice.

Law VIII
The Law of Mastery

A Legacy Author sharpens their craft
continuously.

———————— ✦ ————————

Law Statement:

I will continually improve my skills
and strengthen my craft.

Talent may open doors, but mastery keeps
them open. Without growth, skill fades
and relevance declines. This Law protects
long term effectiveness.

Stopping growth often feels easier than
continuing it. Comfort with current ability
can quietly limit progress. Mastery requires
humility and effort.

Learning, refining, and practicing strengthen your work. Improvement does not happen by accident. It is the result of intentional development.

When you pursue mastery, your confidence grows naturally. Your work becomes stronger, clearer, and more impactful over time.

Law IX
The Law of Advocacy

A Legacy Author believes in their offering.

─────────◆─────────

Law Statement:

I will speak boldly and confidently about my offerings and their value.

If you hesitate to speak about your work, others will notice. Uncertainty weakens trust. This Law exists to confront self doubt.

Belief is not arrogance. It is clarity about value. If your work serves others, it deserves to be spoken about with confidence.

Advocacy connects service to impact. When you clearly express what your work offers, people understand how it helps them.

Strong belief strengthens communication. Confidence invites trust, and trust allows your message to reach those who need it.

Law X
The Law of Partnership

A Legacy Author does not build alone.

───────────── ✦ ─────────────

Law Statement:

I will collaborate, delegate, and
partner to expand my impact.

Trying to do everything yourself limits
growth. Isolation increases pressure
and slows progress. This Law governs
collaboration and delegation.

Partnership does not weaken authority.
It strengthens capacity. Working with others
allows you to focus on what matters most.

Delegation creates space for growth. Collaboration brings new ideas, skills, and reach. Shared effort multiplies results.

When you build with others, your work becomes sustainable. Partnership allows your legacy to extend beyond individual effort.

DAILY EXECUTION STANDARDS
(LAW-ALIGNED)

Law I — Service

Daily Standard:

Serve one person with your message today.

Law II — Alignment

Daily Standard:

Spend time bringing your thoughts into focus before taking action.

Law III — Execution

Daily Standard:

Take at least one action that moves your work forward.

Law IV — Daily Promotion

Daily Standard:

Share your message publicly in some form today.

Law V — Investment

Daily Standard:

Invest time, energy, or resources into your growth today.

Law VI — Declaration
Daily Standard:
Speak clearly about where you are going, not where you are stuck.

Law VII — Courage
Daily Standard:
Do one thing today that feels uncomfortable but necessary.

Law VIII — Mastery
Daily Standard:
Improve one skill connected to your craft.

Law IX — Advocacy
Daily Standard:
Speak confidently about your work and its value.

Law X — Partnership
Daily Standard:
Seek help, collaboration, or support instead of doing everything alone.

THE LEGACY
AUTHOR COVENANT

True Vine L.A.W.S.

I acknowledge that authorship is not only creative expression, but responsibility. I understand that legacy is built intentionally through discipline, alignment, and obedience to principle.

I willingly commit to execute the Ten Laws of the Legacy Author. I accept these Laws as governing standards for how I think, act, promote, invest, speak, and build.

I understand that these Laws are not suggestions. They are commitments that require daily practice and personal accountability.

I commit to create in service, act with discipline, promote with integrity, invest with intention, speak with confidence, grow with courage, improve with humility, advocate with clarity, and build through partnership.

I accept full responsibility for my growth, my actions, and my legacy.

From this day forward, I choose to operate as a Legacy Author.

Author Name (Printed): _____

Signature: _____

Date: _____

www.ingramcontent.com/pod-product-compliance
Lightning Source LLC
Chambersburg PA
CBHW031911200326
41597CB00012B/587